AF269468

# ADVENTURES IN NATURE

# EXPLORING WOODS

BY JEN GREEN AND LIA VISIRIN

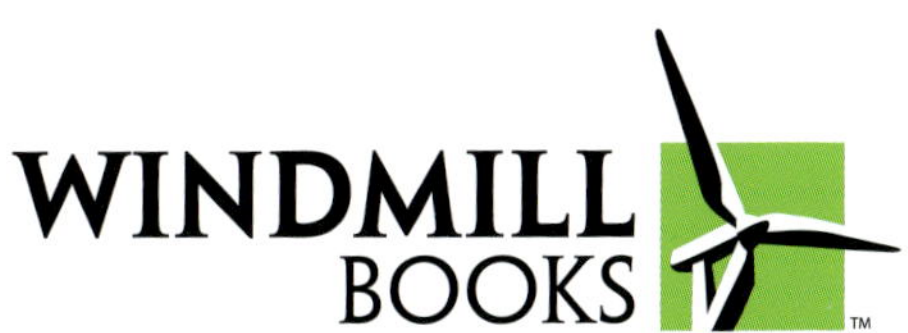

WINDMILL BOOKS

Published in 2026 by Windmill Books,
an Imprint of Rosen Publishing
2544 Clinton St.
Buffalo, NY 14224

First published in Great Britain in 2025 by Hodder & Stoughton
Copyright © Hodder & Stoughton Limited, 2025

Credits
Series Editor: Julia Bird
Series Designer: Peter Scoulding

Cataloging-in-Publication Data
Names: Green, Jen, author. | Visirin, Lia, illustrator.
Title: Exploring woods / Jen Green, illustrated by Lia Visirin.
Description: Buffalo, NY : Windmill Books, 2026. | Series: Adventures in nature |
  Includes glossary and index.
Identifiers: ISBN 9781538398807 (pbk.) | ISBN 9781538398814 (library bound) |
  ISBN 9781538398821 (ebook)
Subjects: LCSH: Forest animals--Juvenile literature. | Forest ecology--Juvenile literature. |
  Nature study--Juvenile literature.
Classification: LCC QH541.5.F6 G743 2026 | DDC 591.73--dc23

All rights reserved.

No part of this book may be reproduced in any form without permission
in writing from the publisher, except by a reviewer.

Printed in the United States of America

CPSIA Compliance Information: Batch #CSWM26
For Further Information contact Rosen Publishing  at 1-800-237-9932

Find us on 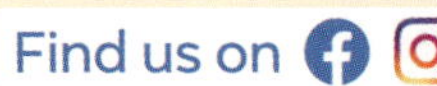

# CONTENTS

# INTO THE WOODS

A wood is a place with many trees growing close together. Woods contain more living things than any other part of the countryside, so they are an ideal place to explore nature! There are two main types of woodland – woods with mainly broadleaved trees and woods with mainly conifer trees.

Conifer trees such as pine, fir, and spruce have narrow, waxy leaves. These trees keep their leaves all year round.

Broadleaved trees such as oak, beech, and chestnut have wide, flat leaves. These trees shed their leaves for winter.

Animals such as foxes, deer, and birds make their home in a wood.

## WHAT TO BRING

When you explore a wood, you will need warm, waterproof clothing, strong shoes, a hat, and sunscreen.

Make notes and drawings using a notebook, pen, and colored pencils. A magnifying glass, camera, binoculars, and a collecting jar will also be useful.

5

# MIGHTY TREES

Trees are the most important plants in a wood. There are many types of tree, but they all have the same parts: leaves, twigs, branches, a thick trunk, and roots.

Each part has a vital job to do. For example, the trunk supports the tree. Roots gather moisture. Leaves use sunlight to make the tree's food.

A tree's trunk and branches hold the leaves high in the air where they can trap sunlight.

Different types of tree have differently shaped leaves. This can help you to identify the tree.

Leaves are like miniature factories. They use water and carbon dioxide gas from the air to make sugary food with the help of the energy in sunlight.

## WHAT DO YOU SEE?

Study a leaf. You should see lines called veins, which carry food and water. Make leaf rubbings by putting paper over different leaves and rubbing the paper with a wax crayon.

Roots anchor the tree. They spread through the soil, sucking up water and minerals.

# PLACES TO LIVE

Trees are like buildings. Animals and plants live at different levels in the tree: high in the leafy layer (canopy), on the trunk, on the ground, or among the roots. The different levels in a tree are called stories, just like the floors in a building.

Squirrels and many birds live high in trees in broadleaved woods. Conifer woods contain less wildlife.

Trees spread their leaves to make a green layer called the canopy.

Insects such as this common blue butterfly feed on woodland flowers.

Trees are the largest living things on Earth! A giant redwood tree can grow to over 330 feet (100 m) tall.

# CHANGING SEASONS

A wood changes constantly as trees and other plants adjust to the seasons. Broadleaved woodlands change more than conifer forests because the trees drop their leaves in autumn. They do this to save energy and keep in moisture.

In spring, days get longer and warmer. Buds open as trees and plants grow new leaves and blossom. Birds build their nests and lay eggs.

Summer brings long, warm, sunny days. Trees are leafy, and there is plenty of food for young woodland animals.

## WHAT DO YOU SEE?

Visit a wood in different seasons. Make notes and drawings of the changes you see. You could photograph your favorite tree or woodland scene in different seasons.

In autumn, the days get shorter and colder. Some birds fly away to warmer places. Trees produce fruits and nuts, then broadleaved trees drop their leaves.

Winter brings cold, frosty days. A wood provides shelter for animals. Dormice spend the winter in a sleep-like state called hibernation.

# HIGH IN THE TREES

Birds, squirrels, and minibeasts live high in the leafy tree canopy. In summer, animals are hard to see among the leaves, but birds such as cuckoos can be identified by their songs.

Birds such as this blackbird nest in trees where their eggs and young are safe from most predators.

Look out for these common woodland birds.

## WHAT DO YOU SEE?

Look for birds high in trees using binoculars. The best time to look is in spring and summer, when birds are busy building nests, laying eggs, and rearing young.

LISTEN OUT FOR BIRDSONG. CAN YOU RECOGNIZE ANY BIRDS FROM THEIR SONG?

# IN THE UNDERGROWTH

The ground below a tree is shaded by the leafy cover above. Plants grow in sunny patches, forming a layer called the undergrowth. Young trees sprout from seeds. These seedlings grow quickly toward the light.

Ferns and other plants grow in patches of sunlight.

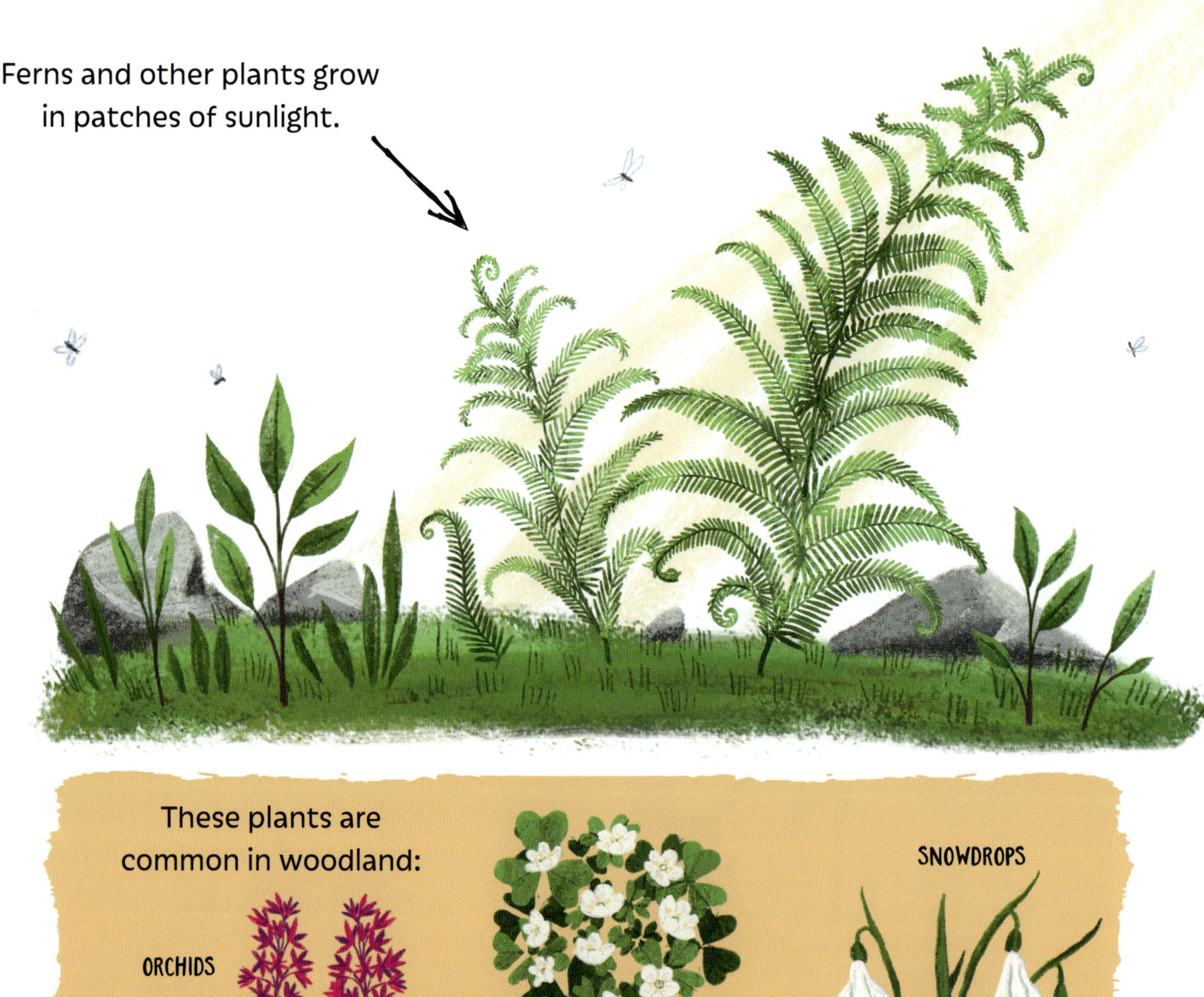

## WHAT DO YOU SEE?

Make a 3-foot (1 m) square on the ground using four pegs and a ball of string. Draw or photograph the plants you see in the square. Use a plant identification book or website to help you identify what you have found.

In spring, wildflowers grow. These bluebell flowers bloom in April and May.

Caterpillars feed on leaves in the undergrowth.

This leaf has been nibbled by insects.

# AMONG THE LEAVES

A carpet of dead leaves covers the woodland floor. Beetles, woodlice, and other minibeasts feed on dead leaves and other organic matter. This helps to break down their remains and return minerals to the soil, to nourish (feed) plants. These small creatures are nature's recyclers!

## WHAT DO YOU SEE?

Study any minibeasts you find using a magnifying glass. Counting the legs can help to identify these creatures. Insects such as beetles have six legs. Spiders have eight. Millipedes and woodlice have many legs. Slugs and worms have none.

A snail's shell protects it from predators and keeps it moist.

*Always wash your hands after touching soil.*

Beetles are insects. All insects have a three-part body with a head, thorax, and abdomen.

Antennae on the head are used for feeling and smelling.

Thorax

The hard wing cases protect the delicate wings.

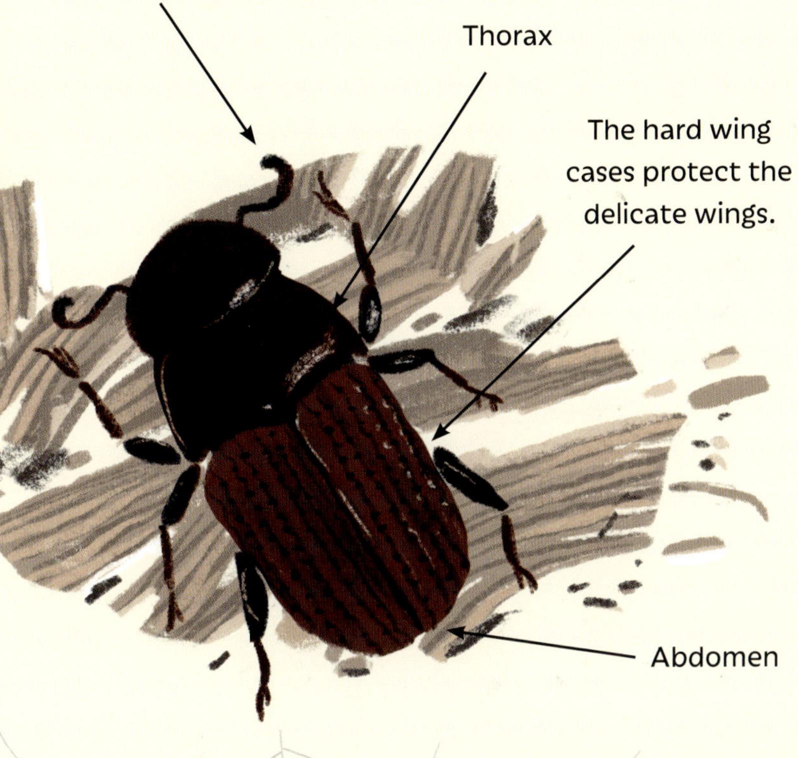

Abdomen

Spiders are arthropods. Some live among woods, where they trap their prey in sticky webs.

# ON A TREE STUMP

Tree stumps and fallen trees are home to all kinds of living things that like moist, dark places. As well as plants such as moss and ferns, there are worms, slugs, and other animals. Mushrooms and toadstools sprout from the stump or roots. These are not plants or animals, but a separate group of living things called fungi.

A tree stump is a mini-habitat for plants such as moss and ivy. Moss soaks up water like a sponge.

Ferns are often found in the damp, shady parts of a wood. They have leafy fronds that uncoil from buds as the fern grows.

Fungi spread by sending tiny spores through the air. They come in lots of different shapes and colors, the most recognizable of which is a toadstool.

Study a tree stump in a wood and the ground around it. Make a list of the things that you find under these headings:

- Plants
- Animals
- Fungi

*Never touch mushrooms or toadstools, as they may be poisonous.*

# IN A CLEARING

A woodland clearing is often sunny and warm in summer. The ground is grassy. Wild flowers attract bees and butterflies. Insects and reptiles such as snakes sunbathe on logs and stones.

Bees visit flowers to sip a sweet liquid called nectar. They also carry dusty pollen from one flower to another, which helps plants to make seeds.

These insects are found in sunny clearings.

Snakes need to warm up in the sunshine to give them energy before they go hunting.

Don't go near wasps, bees, or snakes, as they could sting or bite you.

## WHAT DO YOU SEE?

Butterflies suck up flower nectar using a long tube called a proboscis. If you sit quietly near flowers you may see butterflies sipping nectar with their proboscis.

# FRUITS AND SEEDS

Plants reproduce by making seeds. Many plants make their seeds inside fruits, which can be hard like an acorn, or soft like a cherry. Animals and the wind help to carry seeds far away from the parent plant, where they can sprout and grow.

## WHAT DO YOU SEE?

Autumn is the time to look for fruits and seeds. Soft fruits include apples and blackberries. Chestnut fruits have a spiky case. Fruits with hard shells are called nuts. What fruits and seeds can you find?

Pine trees make their seeds inside cones like these.

Chestnuts

These fruits and seeds are common in woods.

Berries and seeds are eaten by birds and other animals. The seeds pass through them and are dropped in another part of the wood, where some will grow into new plants.

# HIDDEN ANIMALS

Mammals that live in woods include deer, badgers, foxes, hedgehogs, stoats, and squirrels. These animals are shy and very good at hiding! It can be hard to spot them, but signs such as nibbled food and footprints show that they have passed by.



## WHAT DO YOU SEE?

Look for signs of mammals in your local wood, such as fur or droppings. You may find animal footprints in muddy areas. A wildlife book or website will help you to identify the animals. Half-eaten nuts or pine cones may have been nibbled by mice, birds, or squirrels, for example.

Young deer often have a speckled coat which blends in with the shadows. They are called fawns.

Badgers leave piles of earth, stones and grass outside their burrow, which is called a sett.

Never touch animal droppings.

CAN YOU FIND ANY WOODLAND ANIMAL CLUES? DO THEY TELL YOU ANYTHING ABOUT THE ANIMAL'S WAY OF LIFE?

# THE WOODS AT NIGHT

Many woodland animals sleep by day and come out to feed at dusk. Animals that are active at night are called nocturnal. Bats, foxes, badgers, hedgehogs, stoats, and owls are all nocturnal. So are moths, worms, and many other minibeasts.

Night-active animals, like this bat, have senses suited to hunting in darkness.

As it gets dark in a wood, moths and other nocturnal animals appear.

Owls have excellent sight and hearing. They swoop low and catch prey in their sharp claws.



A fox's pricked ears and good eyesight help it to hunt at night.

# NATURE DIARY

Build up a detailed picture of life in a wood by keeping a nature diary. You could collect finds such as leaves and feathers, identify and count trees, or make a map.

## KEEP NOTES

Always take your notebook with you. Record the date, time, weather, and place. Describe what you see. Use drawings, photos, or leaves to illustrate your book.

Note down the shape and color of different flowers and their leaves so you can identify them later using a book or the Internet.

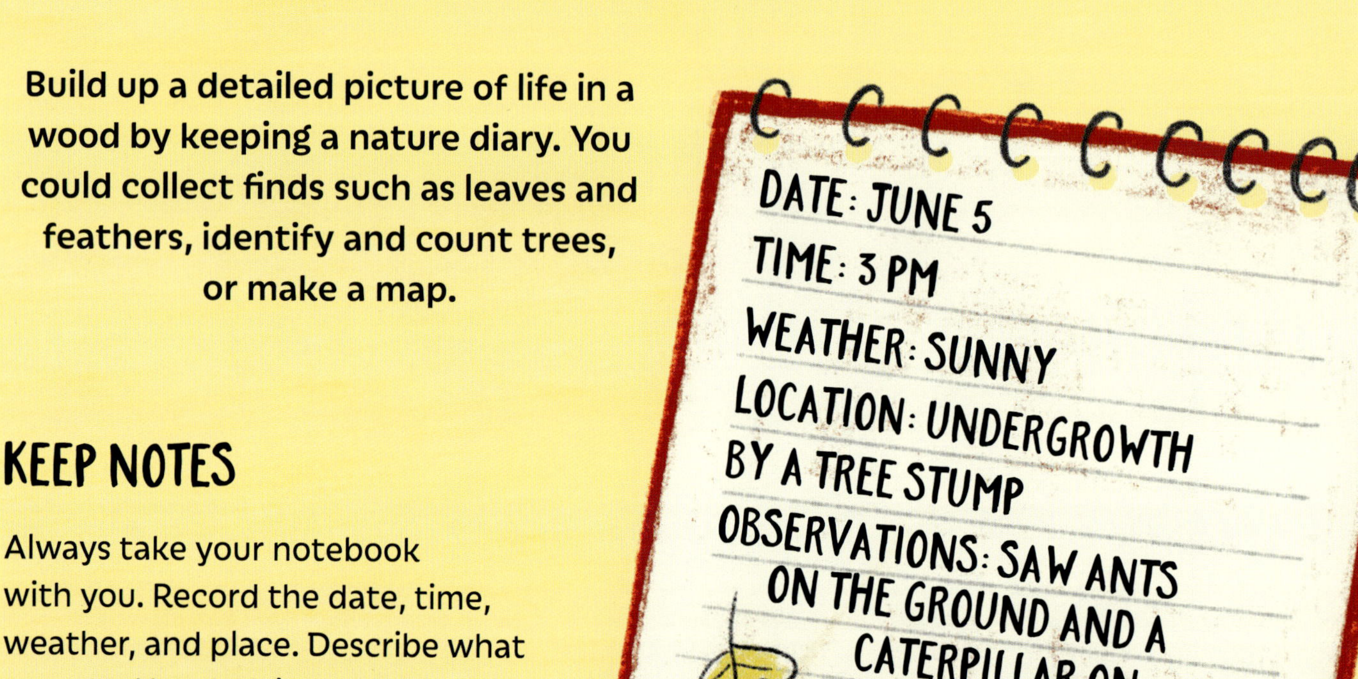

Make a collection of finds such as leaves, feathers, seeds, nuts, and bark. Leaves and feathers can be stuck in your diary.

## TOP TIPS

• Wear green or brown clothes so you blend in with the woods.

• Approach animals with the wind blowing toward you so they don't catch your scent.

• Take a camping mat so you can sit quietly on the ground.

• Don't forget to take care of nature. Always take any litter home with you.

What insect is this? If you see a plant or animal you don't recognize, write notes, take a photo or sketch it. Look it up later in a plant or animal book or online.

## MAKE A MAP

Record all the different trees you find in a small patch of woodland. A tree book or website can help you identify them. Or make a map of the wood, showing habitats such as clearings, streams, and fallen trees.

 *Always be extremely careful near water and stand well away from the water's edge.*

# GLOSSARY

**Antennae** the "feelers" on an insect's head, which are used for sensing.

**Bloom** when flowering plants produce flowers. This usually happens in spring or summer.

**Broadleaved tree** a tree with wide, flat leaves that sheds its leaves in autumn.

**Conifer tree** a tree that keeps its narrow leaves all year round, and produces seeds in cones.

**Drey** a squirrel's nest.

**Fungi** the group of living things that includes mushrooms, toadstools, and mold.

**Habitat** the natural home of plants or animals, such as a wood or a pond.

**Hibernation** a long, deep sleep that some animals go into during the winter season.

**Mammal** an animal with hair on its body, which feeds its young on milk.

**Minerals** the non-living materials of which rocks are made.

**Nectar** a sugary liquid produced by flowers to attract insects.

**Predator** an animal that hunts other animals for food.

**Prey** an animal that is hunted by another.

**Proboscis** the feeding tube of an animal such as a butterfly.

**Reproduce** when plants or animals produce young.

**Seedling** a young tree which has sprouted from a seed.

**Sett** a badger burrow.

**Spore** a cell that can develop into a new seed or fungus.

**Veins** lines that run through leaves, supplying water and food.

# FIND OUT MORE

## Books

*Nature's Classroom: Habitats* by Claudia Martin (Wayland, 2023)

*The Great Outdoors: Woodland* by Lisa Regan (Wayland, 2020)

*The Magic of Forests* by Vicky Woodgate (Dorling Kindersley Limited, 2023)

## Websites

*www.woodlandtrust.org.uk/trees-woods-and-wildlife/animals/*
Discover the animals of the woodland and how they are being protected.

*www.bbc.co.uk/springwatch*
*www.bbc.co.uk/autumnwatch*
Have a look at the BBC's Springwatch and Autumnwatch websites to see how forests and their inhabitants change with the seasons.

*https://www.audubon.org/bird-guide*
Use this helpful bird guide from the National Audubon Society to identify birds in the woods.

NOTE: Every effort has been made by the Publishers to ensure that the websites on page 31 of this book are suitable for children, that they are of the highest educational value, and that they contain no inappropriate or offensive material. However, because of the nature of the Internet, it is impossible to guarantee that the contents of these sites will not be altered. We strongly advise that Internet access is supervised by a responsible adult.

# INDEX

autumn 10, 11, 22

badger 24, 25, 26, 27
bat 26
bee 20, 21
beech tree 4, 6, 7, 9, 29
beetle 16, 17, 20
bird 5, 8, 10, 11, 12, 13, 23, 24
blackbird 12
bluebell 15
broadleaved tree 4, 8, 10, 11
butterfly 9, 21

caterpillar 15
chestnut tree 4, 22, 23
clothes 5, 29
conifer tree 4, 8, 10

deer 5, 24, 25, 27

fir tree 4, 6, 9
flower 9, 14, 15, 20, 21, 28
foliage 12
fox 5, 24, 26, 27
fruit 11, 22, 23
fungi 18, 19

habitat 18, 29
hibernation 11

leaf 4, 6, 7, 8, 10, 11, 12, 13, 14, 15,
    16, 17, 19, 28, 29

mineral 7, 16
minibeast 12, 16, 17, 26

oak tree 4, 6, 7, 23, 29
owl 26, 27

pine tree 4, 22, 24, 29

reproduce 22
root 6, 7, 8, 18

seed 14, 19, 20, 22, 23, 29
snail 16
snake 20
spider 16, 17
spring 10, 13, 14, 19
spruce tree 4
squirrel 8, 12, 13, 23, 24
summer 10, 12, 13, 14, 20
sunlight 6, 7, 14

tree 4, 6, 7, 8, 9, 10, 11, 12, 13, 14, 18, 22,
    23, 26, 28, 29
tree stump 18, 28, 29

vein 7

winter 4, 11, 14, 19